The Challenge of Faith

The Challenge of Faith

by
Br. Francis Maluf M.I.C.M.

Loreto Publications
Fitzwilliam, New Hampshire
A.D. 2004

Cum permissu Ordinarrii,
Episcopal House, Trois-Rivières, Quebec
May 28, 1972. Feast of the Most Holy Trinity

First published by *Éditions Du Bien Public*
Trois-Rivières, Quebec, 1972
Second Edition typeset and
Published by
Loreto Publications
P.O. Box 603
Fitzwilliam, NH 03447
Phone: 603-239-6671
Fax: 603-239-6127
www.LoretoPubs.org

Special thanks to Catherine Rose Hazelrigg for the cover
design and layout.

ISBN: 1-930278-43-8

Library of Congress Control Number: 2004108324

Printed and bound in the U.S.A.

Table of Contents

Editor's Preface

Prayer is a lifting up of the mind and the heart to God by way of adoration, petition, thanksgiving, and/or propitiation. It is a communion of the spirit with its Creator, a worship in spirit and in the truth, an act of humble acknowledgment of the creature's total dependence on God. Those who refuse to pray will not be saved.

Meditation, in the true Catholic sense, is a form of active prayer, not by way of communication with a Divine Person or saint, but by way of reflecting upon God and His Goodness, the Incarnation, or any of the created goods through which one can see the Creator's vestiges, shadows and finite images in things, events and holy persons, and through that applied fixation of the mind glorify Him in our hearts. One does not have to think very hard to meditate; one has to choose a single subject and ponder it intensely in the light of what it declares itself to be and what God intends us to learn from it. Meditation is an intellectual act of invention (in the traditional sense of that word), which is to say that it is a journey of discovery in what may only be fifteen minute excursions.

This is what Brother Francis does so well in these seventy-two concise and scripturally based meditations. Whether it is an event, like the day, or a virtue, like gratitude, or a ravaging infidelity, like Islam, or a person, like Our Lady, he zeroes in on the topic and, with an amazing depth of understanding, simplifies it in relation to time and eternity, and then he examines its relation to each and every man in the larger view of our everlasting destiny. Rarely has one seen the virtues expounded upon with such practical clarity and dynamic energy. Our author emphasizes that everything one experiences day after day in this wayfaring state has the capacity to elevate our human frailty to supernatural heights if we engage in it with the magnanimous attitude of confident sons of God.

The Challenge of Faith is exactly that, a challenge. When it comes to our Lady, for example, there is no soft equivocation. In the spirit of the doctors of the Church, east and west, and with the holy verve of a Louis de Montfort, he cuts to the chase: Devotion to Mary is a sign of predestined election in grace; the lack thereof is a sign of reprobation.

In honor of the seventy-two years our holy Mother Mary Immaculate graced this planet in her mortal state, if any man of desires were to spend a few minutes each morning for that many consecutive days and savor one by one these powerful reflections, that man would be more than an enthusiastic member of the Church Militant; he would be an apostle well prepared for the crowning gift of wisdom; he would be an apostle who has already tasted wisdom's precious precursor and advocate, the gift of understanding.

Brian Kelly
Editor — Loreto Publications

Author's Introduction

Br. Francis Maluf M.I.C.M.

Ideally, these meditations should be read as they were lived: in a few moments of the morning on seventy-two successive days. The seventy-two is in honor of the life on earth of Mary, Queen of Apostles and Mother of the Church. As published here, these notes are the log of a spiritual journey, reproduced with a minimum of editing. The whole is a collection of items of varied lengths, and sometimes of surprising sequence, whose unity is one of life, not of art. The purpose is the formation of an apostle, religious or lay, in the Church Militant.

Faith

1. God created precisely the kind of world in which the act of faith is possible; namely, a world in which God can be sought and found, but also one in which God can be ignored.

2. From our point of view, it is wonderful that God can be found; from God's point of view, it is wonderful that God can hide. It is like hiding a powerful light in a dark room.

3. If God's evidence were equal to His reality, there would be neither love nor merit in our faith.

4. Faith is the knowledge facet of our participation in the divine nature, in our becoming children of God. We know with God's mind realities not connatural to ours: this is what it means to have the Faith.

5. Faith is prefigured by the dark cloud which illumined the night. (Ex. 14:20) It is dark (but that is because it is so far above our nature) and yet it is the only light in the darkness of this life.

6. It is only through faith that we know the cause and meaning of all.

7. Faith is man's first step towards his divine destiny (the Beatific Vision). Failing to take that step is the beginning of the eternal frustration of a life.

Morning Meditations

1. *A custodia matutina usque ad noctem, speret Israel in Domino.* From the morning watch even until night, let Israel hope in the Lord. (Ps. 129:6)

2. I will arise early, I will give praise to thee, O Lord. (Ps. 56:9-10)

3. O God, my God, to thee do I watch at break of day. (Ps. 62:2)

4. The Holy Ghost wants to teach us the beauty and importance of morning meditation.

5. Every day is a new beginning; every day could be our entry into eternity.

6. There are peaks in our lives, moments of spiritual insights and extraordinary graces. Meditation keeps us under the influence of these peaks of grace.

7. The morning meditation could touch every other moment of the day; keep us recollected and in view of our last end.

8. We arouse our powers as from sleep and enkindle the fire of devotion early in the day: ". . .and in my meditation a fire shall flame out." (Ps. 38:4)

9. Morning meditation is to our faculties like the tuning of a musical instrument; during the rest of the day we play our pieces.

10. Like the archer taking his aim, so we fix our eyes on heaven as the objective of all our actions. Like the captain of a ship we ascertain the direction of our course.

11. We comply with the first principle of wisdom: the principle of order – putting first things first. So we start the day by bringing our first fruits to God: our thoughts and acts of love.

12. A slave presents himself to his master or lady, showing that he is ready for any duty.

13. We bring to active life in our minds all the truths of faith which must never perish from the earth.

14. We renew our vows and promises made to God, to our Lady, and to our intimate saints and angels.

15. We refresh our resolutions, and fight against our habitual defects and especially against the sloth of fallen nature.

16. We consider the current problems of our lives in the light of revealed wisdom.

17. We start in our souls a little fire of joy, love, and devotion, and hope that it will burn the rest of the day.

18. *Sicut pullus hirundinis sic clamabo; meditabor ut columba.* (Is. 38: 14) I will cry like a young swallow; I will meditate like a dove.

The Day

1. From the first day of creation the same pattern of day has been repeated. Every entity in existence plays its part in making a day, but the purpose of the day is human.

2. Within the framework of the day every event in history took place, and especially the central and most important event: the work of salvation.

3. Every new day is a fresh beginning, as if God wipes out the past by a good night's sleep and invites us to begin again.

4. Every day could be our last day, and one day is going to be just that.

5. The very monotony of the day's pattern is a challenge to our spirituality, our creativeness, our originality, (which is the signature of person). No one day is exactly like another; no one man's day is like any other man's day. We make our own days as we make our own lives.

6. Every day is a figure of all life and of all time; but the ever repeated cycle of the day is a figure of eternity.

7. Our Lord wants us to be concerned only with today: "Sufficient unto the day is the evil thereof." This is the day of salvation. Am I ready for eternity today?

8. The past and the future are the devil's tools. God is the Eternal Now.

Order

1. The heart of wisdom is the appreciation of order: putting first things first.
2. The mission of religious life is the restoration of order.
3. God created the world for man, and man for salvation: all order serves this one end, the salvation of man.
4. Saint Teresa of Avila commenting on the text, "Thou hast set him over the works of thy hands: Thou has subjected all things under his feet" (Ps. 8: 7-8), says that this is true principally of the saints, because most men subject themselves to the things of this world. Only the saints are truly the lords of creation.
5. Peace is the tranquility of order; beauty is its splendor.
6. Order is the perfect disposition of means to the end. Only those who know the true end can work for order. He who knows not the true doctrines of salvation is like a captain of a ship who does not know the destination of his journey.
7. The only first principle of order is the Apostles' Creed; the best prayer for order is the *Our Father*; the best grasp of the means for order is the *Hail Mary*; the triumphant shout of order is the *Hail Holy Queen*.

Purity

1. Purity is promised the highest reward: "Blessed are the pure of heart for they shall see God." (Matt. 5:8)

2. Purity must spring from the heart, and must pervade every thought, act, or movement.

3. Modesty is the external manifestation of the purity of heart and mind.

4. The beauty of modesty is unforgettable: the greatest spiritual force on earth.

5. The attributes of purity: it is loving, tender, loyal, humble, ardent, and, above all, ferocious — terrible as an army set in array.

6. Purity converted kingdoms and empires, exalted warfare to the sublime status of chivalry, transformed a family, elevated womanhood, and sanctified the earth by the religious vow of virginity.

7. The issues of purity are the personal concern of our Lady: for it is she who made virginity the heart of religion. It is primarily under that aspect that her arch-enemy, Lucifer, studies how to spread in the world the cult of impurity.

8. The triumph of purity is really the victory of the flesh showing the heights to which it can be raised through virtue and grace; it is the greatest achievement of our human nature.

Humility

1. Nothing makes me feel more humble than the consideration of all the times I have been ungrateful or inconsiderate. How many more times I did not even detect myself!

2. Pride and its brood: ambition, arrogance, selfishness, depreciatory thoughts, stubbornness — all are annihilated by childlike obedience.

3. All religious life is a school of humility: poverty is the ground in which it grows, chastity the flower, obedience the stem.

4. Nobody has a better reason to be angry with me than I myself: only God sees us more fully than we see ourselves, i.e., on the inside.

5. The waters of baptism make us children of God! What depth of humility is required to accept this truth and preserve it! How did it reach us through the centuries? By very humble people willing to annihilate all human distinctions and accomplishments in favor of what God does through completely disproportionate means.

6. Before the Incarnation it was the proud and mighty that we considered most God-like; after the Incarnation it is the meek and humble. The difference is Mary. She made lowliness divine.

Chastity

1. Among the flowers of Christian virtue none reflects the beauty of our Lady more perfectly and more personally than the virtue of chastity.

2. It is because of Mary that the state of virginity is exalted as a Christian value — a kind of sweet violence inflicted by the order of grace upon the order of nature. However, we must remember that Christian celibacy involves a new romance . . . higher espousals.

3. Chastity is an angelic virtue and places a higher value on the person, as opposed to the species. The species is immortal in time (the dignity of maternity); the person is immortal in eternity (the dignity of holy virginity). The devil delights to see men deprive themselves of this virtue because, in his view, that places man in his place, so to speak.

4. External modesty is one of the many hedges by which to guard this virtue.

5. Modesty springs from a pure heart and shines in a joyful countenance.

6. Modesty of the eyes is beauty unforgettable. Modest eyes are most eloquent sermons that transform the world. Oh! If only Catholics, and especially Catholic girls, could realize what powerful weapons God has placed at their disposal.

7. Chaste modesty is the love of God by the soul, and the love by God of the soul become visible. It has converted empires; it could still perform miracles.

Poverty

1. The work of Redemption is a romance of poverty. God made us out of nothing; and without Him that is exactly what we still are. But He can still give infinite value to what is of itself worthless. The beloved Saint Francis, *el Poverello*, made this wonderful discovery, and all the saints somehow find it out. It is their secret.

2. Jesus by His own choice was born poor, lived poor, and died poor. He left Himself sacramentally in the Church under the poorest guise. He uses the poorest tools to effect His work: water, oil, bread, and wine. The more insignificant the tool, the more significant is the dignity of the agent. Thus it is that God uses the weak to confound the strong.

3. The spiritual man needs only very few things, but he truly possesses their value with his holy insight.

4. The efficient and successful rich have neither the time nor the insight to contemplate the stars, or to appreciate the flowers of the fields. The poor truly possess the land.

5. The poor man fences his little lot and makes best use of it; the rich let their fences go to ruin and then buy out all their neighbors. The rich own, not land, but abstract power.

6. Our Lord blessed the poor; but poverty is not the same as destitution.

Obedience

1. Poverty is a triumph over the material principle around us; chastity is a triumph over the material principle within us; but obedience is the triumph of our innermost part — a sheer performance of the spirit.

2. All disorder in existence originated in disobedience and continues to spring from it. Lucifer's motto: *Non serviam*, — I shall not obey. Mary's motto: *Ecce ancilla Domini* — I am ready to obey.

3. Obedience is both a command and a counsel: All those who would be saved must obey.

4. Obedience is faith in the will, as faith is obedience in the understanding. The most outstanding attribute of Catholics throughout the centuries is their wonderful obedience . . . some times at what price!

5. Oh! The humility of the obedience of our God! How He obeyed as a child! How He obeys in the Eucharist! and in all the sacraments! Even in answering prayers, He does it as one who must obey!

6. Before the Incarnation all must obey God. Now all must obey like God!

Penitence

1. All virtues are different forms of the love of God; this is evidently true of penitence. Only when we begin to realize the tenderness of God are we overwhelmed with sorrow for all the times we hurt Him by our disloyalty, coldness and grossness.

2. Penitence makes good out of evil: by making our past sins matter for loving God with humility, gratitude, tenderness, holy desires, and firm resolutions for the future.

3. Nothing is worse in spiritual life than callousness.

4. Some people say that what repels them from the Catholic faith is above all the confessional. What a terrible criticism of God, rejecting Him precisely because of His great gesture of mercy! It is like rejecting a medical doctor because he offers remedies.

5. Dearest Saint Mary Magdalen, teach me to make up for my sins by tears, and sorrow, and absolute loyalty to the very end.

Prayer

1. No religious has begun to live religiously until prayer is his most cherished occupation — his most important work.

2. A religious might interrupt his prayer but never the spirit of prayer; he must remain tied to prayer by a strong elastic band.

3. Prayer is association with God and the saints; what exercise would be better preparation for our life in heaven?

4. Those who pray well never fall into heresy. Those who pray sincerely cannot fail to find the way of salvation.

5. Those who pray unceasingly never lose sight of their complete dependence on God; and never fail to correspond to His grace.

6. It is the very issue of faith, that we can achieve more by prayer than by any other kind of activity; indeed, every other kind of activity acquires the virtue of fruitfulness from the overspreading influence of prayer.

7. "But thou when thou shalt pray, enter into thy chamber." (Matt. 6:6) The best places for prayer: my cubicle and Jesus' cubicle.

8. What is Jesus doing in the tabernacle? He reigns invisibly over the earth (but to faith visibly) while communing with the Father and the Holy Ghost.

9. We can pray by looking at Jesus, as Mary did before the cross. The Word Eternal makes our silence eloquent.

10. No activity is good once it becomes a distraction from prayer. Short prayers should salt our entire day: *Fiat voluntas tua* — Thy will be done.

Fasting

1. Fasting is the first discipline of religious life: it places the body under control and asserts the rights of the spirit.

2. It is a principle of chastity and a challenge to sloth.

3. Partial fasting, i.e., leaving the table still hungry, is sometimes more difficult and more meritorious than absolute fasting.

4. A small sign of the cross, a moment for recollection and resolution, are helps to curb the appetite.

5. The spirit of fasting leads to the spirit of consideration and holy conversation.

6. It is amazing how much spiritual value depends on a material act. No angel can fast. It is a challenge to the spiritual spark in our nature to spiritualize the act of eating — knowing all the time how much more God is going to make of this act by instituting the Eucharist. No aspect of our nature can be taken lightly in the light of faith.

Suffering

1. Christianity gave new meaning to old values, like purity, mercy, respect for woman, the ideal of family life; but the greatness of Christianity is in giving value to what was considered bad or pointless, like poverty, humility, work, and above all, death and suffering.

2. There is no sanctity without suffering. Those who lack a realization of this truth have not yet reached the alphabet of spiritual life.

3. The cross is the signpost on the highway to heaven.

4. It is only through suffering that we begin to understand Jesus and to imitate the saints. Show me the saint who did not suffer.

5. To take up our cross and follow Jesus was not an invitation to a few. It is the condition of being Christian — a disciple of Christ.

6. Theology, professions of faith, preaching, all these can become vacant sounds, unless marked with the sign of the cross, the stamp of suffering.

Patience

1. Patience is the daughter of charity and the mother of peace — the queen of every happy society.

2. Men are, at one and the same time, each other's delight and mortification. This is true even (rather it is true especially) of those who love and are loved.

3. When God does not seem to hear our prayers, He gives us the privilege of this golden virtue. Yes, even with God! (What daring! What almost blasphemy!) Even with God, we have at times to be patient. Yet how good it is for us to remember His patience with us!

4. How often have I been the mortification of those who love me!

Vigilance

1. In war every soldier is responsible for only the space within the scope of his senses and of his weapons; but within this region, the soldier is the army, indeed, the whole kingdom. At least in one little spot everything depends on him. He alone must, in one limited area, find out all that may serve or hinder the cause of victory. He has to be constantly on the alert. Every object or event must be evaluated quickly and intelligently in terms of victory or defeat with a corresponding plan of action.

2. Because man can be distracted or fall to sleep, God, in the battle for salvation, has assigned for us guardian angels. In that battle vigilance can never be relaxed.

3. The devil never goes to sleep; and his human agents are constantly on the *qui vive,* on the alert.

4. Vigilant soldiers are often persecuted by their own, for seeing signs of danger where the less vigilant see nothing at all.

5. In this life there is no peace, and no victory is final. Otherwise, we would not be the Church Militant.

6. When the soldiers of Christ forget that the war is on, we seem to have achieved peace. What has really happened is defeat for the Faith and surrender to the powers of darkness.

7. We have a subtle enemy; one who can see us but whom we cannot see!

8. Religious are night guards: they watch for the whole city when all are asleep.

9. Close to the end of time, even the elect will be almost deceived. The need for vigilance is on the increase.

10. Our Lady did not go to sleep during the night of the Agony. If we ask her she can obtain for us the grace of great vigilance.

Determination

1. Saint Teresa speaks of the disappointment felt by a person when a friend, having made him a gift, comes and takes it back. A child feels this injury in a special way.

2. A gift, to be pleasing, must be generously given: not hesitantly but cheerfully and firmly.

3. Saint Bonaventure names caution, *cautela*, among the primary effects of the devil's influence in the world. Who could estimate how many vocations and inspirations to great holy deeds were extinguished in souls by this *cautela*, unholy caution? Every act of faith strikes at this diabolic hindrance.

4. God instituted matrimony as a symbol of unqualified incautions, and determined giving of self. When this attribute is taken away, matrimony ceases to be what it was meant to be by God. All the beauty, chivalry, tenderness, of Christian family life are rooted in this quality of the Christian marriage contract. But this is only the symbol of the greater espousals in religious life.

5. As soon as the devil sees hesitancy, he spies an opportunity.

6. "Why hesitate!" says Saint Teresa, "What is to be lost? When you find by experience the tenderness of God, you will know what I mean." She stakes all her authority on this one point: "If you find me wrong in this, don't take anything else I say."

7. When you give a child a toy, let him use it as he likes, or even leave it alone.

8. God was given to us as a child, and as a child receives our gifts.

Fortitude

1. Saint Teresa says that the devil is afraid of resolute souls. Fortitude is not only a virtue, but the backbone of all virtue.

2. Fortitude is sometimes harder in small matters than in big ones, and in spiritual matters than in physical ones. There are many people who dare every kind of danger, but very few who dare to think the truth about the most important matters — even in the secrecy of their own minds.

3. The two pillars of chivalry: purity and fortitude — they could transform the earth.

4. Even in the natural order, without fortitude nothing is achieved.

5. Fortitude is the bridge between us and our ideals.

6. Where could we find a greater teacher of fortitude than the Crucifix!

Liberty

1. The faithful live in the universe like children in their Father's house, enjoying the liberty of the sons of God.

2. Liberty is a Christian value defended by dogma. It is part of religion, but it is not the whole. Those who try to make it the whole (that is, the Liberals) end by destroying its very grounds: truth and morality.

3. Tyranny and oppression are helpless in the face of those who know their duty towards God: the duty to know the truth and to say it. They can kill the body of man, but the liberty of man they cannot touch.

4. When the individual is free to make his own religion and his own morality, society must choose between anarchy and oppression.

5. Our Lord was often paradoxical but never untrue. "You shall know the truth", He said, "and the truth will make you free". (John 8:32) Freedom is the effect, not the cause, of possessing the truth.

6. There is no worse tyranny than that of the "Liberals" in power.

Work

1. Work is not merely a penitential discipline in our fallen state, but also a challenge to our creativity — an instrument of great joys. Even for its penitential aspect, we ought to be extremely and piously grateful.

2. The members of the Holy Family, and after them the saints, have exalted labor to a new dignity.

3. The Catholic religion mentions work, with study and prayer, as tools of sanctification. This is the greatest constructive force of Christian civilization.

4. It is God who made work a necessity for this life, and only God could have made it avoidable. No one else can. No one else should try.

5. God blesses work but not oppression; work creates and is joyful; oppression distorts the victim, but even more, the one who inflicts it.

6. For the spiritual man, the needs of life are few. Our undisciplined desires are often our oppressors.

7. In the beginning there was no slavery. Slavery arose when man's natural desire for infinite happiness was replaced by an infinite desire for finite things.

8. It is religious discipline which alone restores the beauty of work and the beauty of leisure: the two parts of happiness on earth.

9. Slavery is a state in which all one's work is for another, and all one's leisure is from another. It is beautiful when that other is God or the Mother of God.

10. Love makes work joyful; thought makes it fruitful.

11. Perfect happiness is not for this life; but there is a kind of happiness meant for this life, and it belongs to those who are working for their eternal happiness. The way to heaven is the only heaven on earth.

12. Here are some of the joys and conquests of work: to make the desert fruitful, to bring order out of chaos, to tame the passions, to subdue a rebellious nature, to make up for sins, to render charity tangible, to make of ordinary routine life a romance.

13. With the weakening of the Faith, work lost its contemplative spark and gravitated back to mere servility; Christians ought to work with the liberty of the sons of God.

Defeatism

1. With us in the Church Militant there are those who are unaware of the magnitude and seriousness of the battle, of the weaknesses in our ranks, and of the hidden forces behind the enemy; but there are also those who know enough about these things to be discouraged. The latter are worse than the first, because to be discouraged is a practical denial of God. The shout of our God proclaiming: "I have overcome the world!" (John 16:33) still echoes in the land.

2. The cruel, cold, Masonized, Jewish-controlled, faithless world of our time must be conquered the way the early Christians won over the Roman Empire. Saint Agnes and Saint Cecilia were not defeatists.

3. The faith must be professed whether encouraged and protected by the secular power, or crushed and persecuted by it. The twelve Apostles did not move into a friendly world, opening their arms to receive them. Being disciples of Jesus, they expected and welcomed the treatment He received.

4. Our confidence is due to the omnipotence of God; the devil is powerful, but not omnipotent.

5. All the holy angels and all the saints are fighting for our side in the battle of salvation. Were it not for the little darkness that always accompanies the faith, there would almost be no merit in fighting for it.

6. If only we could convince Catholics that when they utter the sentences of the Creed, they are asserting simple facts: the greatest truths that could be uttered on earth "I believe in God the Father *Almighty* . . ."

Perseverance

1. Saint Teresa of Avila warns that we sometimes get discouraged just when we have almost arrived. *"Podra ser que ya que no os falta sino bajaros a beber, lo dejeis todo."*

2. The darkest moment often precedes the break of dawn.

3. The true penitent does not despair, because he depends not on his own strength but on the grace of God.

4. Saint Teresa talks about lowering ourselves to drink. We expect celestial water to rain down from heaven, but since the Incarnation, we are more often surprised to find it springing up from the lowest places of earth.

Mortification

1. Success! Progress! Advancement! Riches! Power! Popularity! Influence! Rising in society! Raising the standard of living! — How can a man stare at a crucifix and continue to use the vocabulary of worldly wisdom!

2. All good came to men from the Cross: a symbol of death, shame, defeat, frustration!

3. The sign of the Cross is the mark of a Christian. What does it mean unless it is the external sign of a mortified life?

4. There were many people surrounding our Lady at the Feast of Cana, but only a few at the foot of the Cross.

5. Levity is the mark of our age: our world is a complete contradiction of the spirit of mortification, external as well as internal.

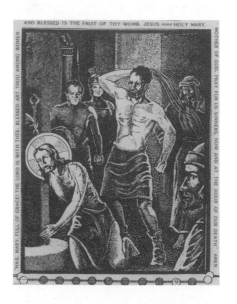

Fervor

1. Our God is a consuming fire. (Heb. 12: 29) I am come to cast fire on the earth. (Luke 12: 49) Once we are caught in that fire, our life becomes transformed, and also all of our values. Our energy becomes positive rather than negative — an adventure rather than a process of disentangling.

2. The Rosary is a sign of fervor and a cause thereof. It is the incarnation of fervor in devotional life. Without fervor we cannot utter its words or think its thoughts.

3. Like fire, fervor cannot remain hid; its external manifestations are: eagerness, enthusiasm, ardent charity, graceful modesty, desire to help others and make them happy.

Hope

1. We only begin to hope when we begin to hope in God, and not in our own strength, and not in anything of this world.

2. Hope is humility: knowledge of self and of the goodness of God.

3. Hope is the most appropriate virtue for our life *in via*. It is the core of piety, the soul of spiritual life.

4. Hope lifts our hearts to heaven, and is mirrored in our eyes. "Hear us, O God, our Savior, the hope of all the ends of the earth." (Ps. 64: 6) The world knows no other hope except what springs from our Faith.

5. Saint Augustine saw a necessary order of dependence in the three theological virtues: no hope without faith, and no charity without both.

Holy Joy

1. True joy must have foundations in reality. The foundations of holy joy are the mysteries of the Rosary. If we can keep our minds and hearts on them, we shall never lose our joy.

2. Sufferings, disappointments, persecutions, frustrations, contradictions, insults, the low opinion of others, lack of consideration, coldness: all these are permitted by God as a challenge to the virtue of holy joy.

3. Holy joy is the outpouring of devotion, the measure of faith.

4. Holy joy must flow from the highest supernatural fountainheads. When we fail to kindle a virtue from inside, we can always try to start from the outside: one short prayer or ejaculation, or a little work of faith, can often be the spark.

5. Holy joy is the radiance produced by the presence of the other virtues in the soul.

6. When the utterance of the Holy Names of Jesus, Mary and Joseph fail to put joy in our hearts, there is something wrong with our faith.

7. All actions which proceed from motives of faith and charity restore peace and joy to the soul.

Peace

1. Peace is the tranquility of order and the genuine manifestation of religious virtue.

2. When we realize that the will of God has been ruling the universe since the day of creation and will continue to rule it after we are gone, that victory is already guaranteed and prophesied, that our only legitimate worry is to see to it that we are on the side of victory; it is then that we begin to do our immediate daily duties leaving the issue to God. In this is peace.

3. Peace is a necessary condition for growth. All the processes of life require peace as a necessary condition – *conditio sine qua non*.

4. Violence by its very definition is contrary to nature. Natural forces proceed sweetly — disturbances are ultimately traceable to the original disturbance, the *Non serviam* of Lucifer. Nothing could be sweeter than a flower growing from day to day. The forces of grace work even more sweetly.

5. Grace becomes violent only in order to overcome the sloth of nature or to punish its deviations. There is, however, a sweetness that accompanies the violence of grace, in contradistinction to every other form of violence.

6. The kingdom of heaven is taken by violence but retained in peace — a new kind of peace, not as the world giveth.

7. The first disturbance was Lucifer's revolt; that state of war which was then begun entered our human order by the first human act of disobedience.

8. The first duty for every one of the faithful (especially for every religious) is to restore peace in his own little disordered world; but since the issue of peace is one and universal, every such victory or realization touches the universal war. Every little campaign is part of the total strategy.

Generosity

1. Cheerfulness in sacrifice is the mark of generosity. This is why God loves the cheerful giver.

2. When God seems to ignore us and disregard our prayers, He seems to be ungenerous; but we know this cannot be true. This is the time He tries our generosity — how much we mean our promises.

3. God knows how to make our frustrations fruitful in ways we do not know. Heaven will be a surprise!

Detachment

1. Detachment from the world is attachment to God and to the things of God. Hence, it is a grace of the Holy Ghost, Who alone can set our desires in order.

2. When we begin to love being recollected in God, we begin to reveal our predestination to heaven. No external circumstance can disturb us after that.

3. No tyrant, no power on earth, can take away from us the spirit of prayer, or our love of recollection, any more than they could take away our faith and our trust in God. My only real and dangerous enemy is myself: I can throw away all eternity in a second!

4. Detachment is wisdom. Wisdom is happiness. Happiness is peace.

5. The sign of the Cross can only mean detachment. The Cross is the divide between us and those attracted by things temporal. They go one way; we go another.

6. "Thyself alone, O Lord!" —Saint Thomas Aquinas.

Abandonment

1. The first attribute of childhood: abandonment to the care of others; frank avowal of our needs.

2. All those who love Saint Thérèse seek occupations and duties consonant with the state of spiritual childhood — opposite to what the world ambitions.

3. When we act thus we can claim from our Lady her full mother's care and protection.

4. It is thus also that we remain true clients of Saint Thérèse.

Recollection

1. Recollection is a prerequisite to all prayer. It is the first discipline of spiritual life. The world as such is the realm of distraction. Every true good begins in a moment of recollection.

2. The *Our Father* is a prayer of recollection (when prayed thoughtfully); so is the *Hail Mary*. The people of the world are praying for recollection when they repeat these two prayers. All that remains is for them to cooperate with the grace which is sure to be given — the grace to withdraw momentarily from the distractions of the world and to think about salvation.

3. Saint Teresa grounds recollection on the realization that God (and therefore also heaven) is within us.

4. Distraction comes from seeking happiness in other things.

5. To be upset by what people think of us is itself a distraction.

6. To place our hope for happiness in anything we do externally is another.

7. A sign and cause of recollection: closing our eyes or running to our cubicles, or even better, to Jesus' cubicle — the chapel.

8. Eternity overarches all of time.

Meditation

1. Blessed is the man of meditation, for he is constantly guided by the "great thought" of eternity. He walks on the earth like a spiritual giant.

2. Those who have never acquired the habit and art of meditation live on the outside of things. — This is true especially in regard to religion.

3. Like a blind man in a garden of flowers is the one who does not meditate.

4. What thundering truths are compressed in the simple words of the Creed! And yet we repeat them like parrots, or like a child counting his marbles without much thought.

5. The "Amen" at the end of the Creed means: These things are really so. We would live in a different world were men to meditate on the Creed.

Grace

1. Grace makes us attractive to heaven, as beauty makes us attractive to earth.
2. Saint Teresa of Avila says that men advise a woman to study the tastes of her spouse and conform herself to him in order to make a success of their marriage; and this even if the husband is a bad man. How much more ought we to study the tastes of Jesus and Mary and conform ourselves to them in our religious life!
3. The children of this world are wiser in seeking what seems to be good!
4. All things naturally desirable have their counterparts in the order of grace; thus:

In the Order of Grace

Glory in heaven
Virtue and grace
The gifts of the Holy Ghost
Membership in the communion of saints
Militancy for the faith (The missions)
The charismata of the Apostles
The fruits of the Holy Ghost
Eternal merits
Being heirs to the kingdom of heaven and sons of God
Salvation

In the Order of Nature

Fame on earth
Health and beauty
Worldly prudence
Status in society
Sports and adventure
Influence
Education
Riches and possessions
Fortunate inheritance
Success

Gratitude

1. The state of grace is one of mutual gratitude between God and us. Indeed, God is excessively grateful to those who cooperate with His graces; He also is very much hurt by lack of gratitude — "Where are the nine?" (Luke 17:17)

2. Sadness is a mark of lack of gratitude. The saints are always radiant with joy — a reflection of their realization and appreciation of God's benefits.

3. The prayers of thanksgiving are especially recommended in Holy Scripture.

4. Our gratitude to God should include also those through whose means God deals with us, and guides our journey: our patron saints, our guardian angels, our superiors, as well as our companions *in via*.

5. The saints eagerly extended their gratitude to include even their persecutors. We must resist the enemies of God who hinder the cause of salvation; but we must thank God for our enemies as an opportunity to suffer persecution for His sake.

6. As long as we stand firm in our faith and persevere in the state of grace, there is no limit to the number of persons we must be grateful to, or the number of benefits and good things we must be grateful for.

Helpfulness

1. The first law of happiness: seek to make others happy.

2. God made the world such that we can never run out of the occasions to serve others.

3. In a religious community the happiness of one nourishes the happiness of all — we *are* our brother's keeper.

4. This is especially true in our community, which was formed and subsists in a state of siege. Even the physical safety of each individual is guarded by the loyalty of all. This makes every loyal brother or sister a sacred person and a precious thing.

5. Even people in the world are promised the eternal rewards of heaven for a glass of water offered in the name of an apostle, that is, one occupied in preserving and spreading truths of the Faith.

Sloth

1. Sloth is an open invitation to all vices.

2. Sloth is the inertia of nature resisting supernatural life. Therefore, some extremely active people are yet truly slothful.

3. Only when we realize what we can earn and merit in our supernatural life can we realize the ugliness of sloth.

4. It helps in combating sloth to be dressed and equipped for action. *Sint lumbi vestri praecincti et lucernae ardentes in manibus vestris.* "Let your loins be girt, and the lamps burning in your hands." (Luke 12: 35) The kings used to go to sleep in full armor.

38

Folly

1. To God in eternity, the challenge in creating did not consist in making a world in which He, Who is infinite light, should be knowable to an intelligent creature, but rather in creating a world in which He could hide.

2. Considered from this point of view, even the folly of atheism gives glory to God. Omnipotence, so to speak, was able to face up to the challenge!

3. God's relative hiddenness in our world constitutes a game of love; and love can and will discover.

4. Only the fool says in his heart: "There is no God"; (Ps. 13:1) but it is a greater folly still, having known God, not to serve Him as God.

5. It seems that, sometimes, God makes the lesser fool punish the greater one.

Thought

1. Thought is the leading principle of human action. Penance is essentially a change of thought (*metanoia**). We can be made holy by switching to holy thoughts.

2. This is why the doctrines of Faith are the irreplaceable foundations of Christian life and culture. Tampering with ideas is the first phase of all revolutions.

3. Catholic doctrine is truth and condemns all deviation from it as error.

4. Knowledge of truth alone is constructive thought. Error as such is subversive.

5. The body of Catholic doctrine is something both divine and human, and as such is a faithful image of the God-man. As divine it rests on the highest authority. As human it is adapted to our manner and employs all our powers; it is preserved largely by human methods and is defended by human weapons.

6. All constructive thought tends towards one objective: the victory of the Faith throughout the whole world. Humility is to admit that the knowledge of salvation (true wisdom) can come only from God. It is a sufficient dignity for the human mind that is capable of being a receiver of this wisdom. In this consists the thin line between presumption and despair.

7. Man is not left free before God to make his own religion, or even to choose his own religion. Man is left free to discover for himself the one true religion, that is, physically free, with salvation and damnation in the stakes.

* In the Greek text of the gospels, *metanoiete* is the inspired word used in translating the Aramaic for the plural imperative "[you] do penance". *Meta* means change. *Noia* (from *nous*) means mind.

8. The acts of faith must not be, cannot be, coerced; but the right of the true faith to be proclaimed must be protected sometimes even by force of arms.

9. It may sound paradoxical to say that men before God are free only to think the truth, but the same paradox challenges us in our Lord's statement: "You shall know the truth, and the truth will make you free." (John 8: 32)

10. Thought is the seed of eternity in us; our ultimate happiness is the fulfillment of thought.

Memory

1. Memory is the greater part of personality, the index of love, the depository of wisdom, the determinant of virtuous action, the effective and abiding part of education.

2. All the original and creative works of mind and imagination presuppose the cooperation of memory, and are enriched by its available treasures.

3. For a sound educational policy, the discriminate employ of the memory is of paramount importance. There ought to be an objective, common, ordered body of knowledge to be universally conveyed; but it ought to be kept to the essential minimum, to be completed by personal choice. Excessive and burdensome use of the memory may eventually crush personality, discourage the weak, eliminate the functions of all the other faculties, and make learning loathsome.

4. It is of the essence of memory to be selective: it would be monstrous to remember everything.

5. It is a great mystery why we remember some very small matters.

6. Memory is the heart's treasure house.

7. There is a law of the divine economy (amply confirmed in my personal experience): We do not quickly forget matters bearing on our own salvation.

8. The abundance of a man's heart — that is memory.

Wisdom

1. Wisdom is knowledge (for the wise man is, above all, one who knows) but it is not mere knowledge. A man could acquire all knowledge and be a fool.

2. As knowledge, wisdom is its greatest perfection, and that in every respect. One instance of knowledge can be greater than another by virtue of the importance of the thing known, or the resulting happiness in the one knowing, or the depth of union between the two. On all these scores wisdom excels all other forms of knowledge.

3. Wisdom is knowledge of the most important matters in the most perfect manner. It is ordered, stable, penetrating, profound, reaching to what is primal.

4. It is only when the appearances have led us to the fountainhead of all existence that we become wise.

5. The wise man is one in whom there is a total inclination to the Good. Knowledge is only one facet of the gem of wisdom.

6. Knowledge is wisdom only inasmuch as it leads to God. The wise are truly godlike.

7. True wisdom can only come from God, and can also be withdrawn by Him. Therefore, the life of wisdom is continual prayer.

8. Philosophy is universal but abstract; experience is concrete but unordered; science is ordered but narrowing; opinion is liberal but unstable. Wisdom is universal and concrete, ordered and liberal (ennobling, contemplative). Wisdom is simple and versatile, penetrating and firm. It is clear without being trivial, deep without being obscure.

9. Wisdom is seeking the things that count. Only the saints are truly wise.

Philosophy Part One

1. If one common error has been the use of philosophy as a substitute for religion, an equally pernicious error is the use of revelation to suppress thought.

2. Without revelation there is no faith, and without philosophy, no civilization.

3. God revealed to us the duty to adore, but not how to build churches.

4. Man, being in the image of God, must remain in a sense a creator; God respects that, even loves it. To create, man must think correctly — be a philosopher.

5. We must do our part in building the City of God on earth. The work must be human as well as divine. This is the divine policy.

6. The Church traditionally has been the guardian of culture and the champion of liberal education. To teach men to think deeply and correctly, to combat error, and to introduce order in thought will always be part of the mission of the Church Militant. These things are needed for the work of salvation.

7. Sound morality, just laws, norms of excellence in art, and especially, orthodoxy in matters of religion are rooted in deep philosophic principles, and will not long flower without these.

8. Give the Faith to a barbarian and he will begin to dress modestly, act soberly, think clearly, and cultivate the arts of civilization.

9. Take the Faith away from highly civilized peoples and they begin to revert to savagery and to degenerate to softness and cruelty.

10. The only true liberty is of those who freely guard the truth.

Philosophy Part Two

1. Philosophy is not a substitute for religion, but its prime minister, i.e., its first servant.

2. All error is contrary to faith, yet every secondary truth can be a distraction.

3. Philosophy keeps the mind open towards the primary and the ultimate.

4. Science, left to itself, tends to complexity and leads to all sorts of monisms. Philosophy, ruling the sciences, tends towards simplicity and completeness of vision. There are many monistic sophistries (oversimplifications of reality) but true philosophy has a place for every grade and aspect of being.

5. When true philosophy is not cultivated, either the natural activities of the mind are stifled at their highest functions or false philosophies arise. Truly nature, in this respect, abhors a vacuum.

6. Philosophy prepares the mind for revelation: it does not give all the answers, but it asks all the questions.

7. True philosophy defends the Faith against sophistry and error.

8. Philosophy provides the Faith with an accurate language with which to express, to teach, and to preserve the *depositum fidei*, the deposit of faith.

9. The sure mark of sound philosophy is humility in the face of revelation — the true meaning of self knowledge, as interpreted by the wisest of philosophers.

Science

1. All things contribute to the glory of God, even science, the marvel of the modern age.

2. When we contemplate what scientists have done and are doing, we gaze at an astounding aspect of God's most wonderful creature, and we praise God. Yet so many scientists do not contemplate and do not praise.

3. Certainly the very reality of the sciences and the inventions of science are a striking testimony of the mastery of mind over matter, and an emphatic assertion of the reality of the spiritual; yet so many scientists use their most spiritual power (their intellect) to deny the reality of the spiritual.

4. It is the tragedy of the modern age that scientists on the whole have not been as grateful to their Creator as they might have been. The coldness of this generation is at least partly due to that.

5. By their very method and approach, most scientists commit themselves to a restricted view of the material aspect of things, to a utilitarian approach which stifles the contemplative interest.

6. How could the scientists decide for or against the revealed account of creation? Creation involves a free act of an omnipotent power. By the nature of the case, creation is not a phenomenon that can be controlled, measured or repeated. The scientists must assume (as scientists) that things always happen in the manner of the phenomena before their eyes.

7. God uses miracles in order to authenticate the supernatural order, and intelligent but simple men have always learned the lesson intended by miracles. But the scientist can only relegate miracles to the class of things "we do not yet understand."

8. Human intelligence has always, and almost unanimously, concluded to the existence of God, from the consideration of the universe which we all experience in common. Some reach this conclusion simply and swiftly in the manner of a child, and some methodically and cautiously in the manner of the philosopher.

9. Holy Scripture teaches us that man is reprehensible when he cannot reach even without the assistance of divine revelation a knowledge of God, of "His eternal power and divinity." (Rom 1:20)

10. The Christian missionary is not sent to preach the existence of God. He should be able to take that for granted. The apostle is to bring the good news of God-become-man, and the consequences of that great event for our human destiny.

11. But the scientist, chained to his ideology and to his method, can be, and often is, indefinitely distracted from ever finding God. In place of the primacy of the first cause he can be lost in an infinity of secondary causes, and, instead of reaching the fullness of eternal being, he is left with the emptiness of an indefinitely long duration of time.

The Issue

1. There is one central and unifying issue of the entire human story. From the fall of our first parents to the last day of time, all human activities are somehow related as either helping or hindering the work of redemption.

2. Sacred history provides the only true picture: the core and the periphery of human things.

3. It is part of the Faith to possess such a unifying conception of history. It is within that perspective that the most challenging, but also the most comforting, doctrine of the Faith (the particular providence of God) becomes evident.

4. It is not remarkable that things in history change; but it is remarkable that there are people today who hold the same faith as that held by Abraham, Noe, and Adam. It is more remarkable that the object of hope and desire of those patriarchs is now a historic fact, indeed, a central fact of history.

5. All merely temporal issues will amount to exactly nothing in an interminable eternity; events can acquire permanent significance only as they bear on the salvation of persons.

6. There exist only two spiritual (and therefore invisible) kingdoms at war for our souls, and we must end up in one or the other.

Idolatry

1. Idolatry as such was virtually dead at the instant God died on the cross. It was then that the idols of earth lost their mystical power; and after that, whenever idolatry confronted the faith of Christ, it offered little or no religious opposition. In the present age, the main resistance to the true religion is to be found in theosophy and iconoclasm. One denies the uniqueness of the Incarnation, and the other denies the fact.

2. In the Temple of Jerusalem the angels were represented visibly for veneration. They were, in that epoch, the only creatures in the beatific vision.

3. Idolatry localizes holiness, and in that respect alone it does express a true religious instinct in man, meant to await the Incarnation.

4. The idols of our epoch are, on the whole, things of the mind: science, art, progress, and a legion of similar ideologies.

5. The cult of ancestry is another form of idolatry still very much with us. I wonder if this cult cannot be considered as the greatest single hindrance to the spread of the faith.

6. Inordinate loyalty to one's ancestors, even where truth and salvation are concerned, ought to be a force working occasionally in favor of the true faith, namely, where the faith is the ancestral tradition. But God sees to it that it never gets to be just that. Every generation of Catholics, indeed every individual Catholic who survives to the age of reason, must make his own act of faith.

7. We do not go to heaven on the faith of our ancestors.

The Jews

1. No man is wise who does not think correctly about the Jews. On this subject it is very easy to be wrong, and there are many different varieties of errors into which to fall.

2. They are a unique type of collectivity — a matter for history, not for sociology.

3. Every one knows that the Jewish problem is unique, and the Jews make use of the fact when it works to their advantage.

4. Their election in the Old Testament, which we must accept on faith, is at least as mysterious as their rejection in the New Testament. The Jews are willing to take the first part of the bargain, which they did not deserve, but not the second, which they did.

5. Many nations were converted by one apostle; our Lord Himself failed with the Jews.

6. It is very difficult for us to understand why God should have favored them as much as He did, yet the Faith somehow survived in their midst, through a line of living traditions which was at times extremely thin.

7. The whole fact of the Jewish reality is a miracle of divine intervention. How did Holy Scripture survive in their keeping, with all that it says about them? How did the expectation of the Savior to come remain the core of their life and the topic of their ordinary conversations? Even the faithless and the wicked among them could tell you when and where He was to be born, as did the scribes and the Pharisees when Herod inquired of them.

8. No other people was equally favored; no other people more stubbornly resisted. Jesus says of them: "They will not believe, even if a man were to rise again from the dead." (Luke 16:31)

9. A true, firm, and unsentimental understanding of the Jewish problem is absolutely necessary for one who must protect the Faith and the faithful. The higher the responsibility, the greater the necessity.

10. Ever since the moment of the Crucifixion, the Jews are engaged in a mystical war against the Church, but they are only effective when the Faith is weak.

Zionism

1. Zionism is the logical consequence of the rejection of Jesus Christ as fulfillment of the Old Testament.

2. Mount Sion is where the Blessed Sacrament was instituted, and where the Holy Ghost descended on the first community of believers to make them the beginning of the Church. The seers of the Old Testament talk enthusiastically about Sion because they saw these realities in prophetic vision. To give to those old prophecies the Zionist interpretation is to inflict the maximum distortion on God's merciful plan for the good of all nations.

3. Every form of heresy is a contribution to the Zionist cause. So is every kind of schism. The papacy is the appointed guardian of the highest interests of the nations.

4. Zionism can win only by dominating and subverting the Christian order.

Government

1. The spirit of rebellion is on the march in the world today, but rebellion as such is against God, from whom all power and all authority descend.

2. Our first impulse towards government ought to be one of gratitude. It stands between us and chaos. It is a necessary condition for the apostolic activity of the Church. So was the Roman Empire for the first apostles, even when they had to pay with their blood in order to resist its encroachments and its oppression. We never hear of the Apostles organizing a rebellion against the government of any country in which they labored.

3. Tyranny is often permitted by God, a punishment for the general attitude of disloyalty to the Faith.

4. Those who free themselves from the sweet yoke of Christ will suffer their necks to bear the yoke of man and of Satan.

5. The saints are the best friends of the people, the most effective guards against oppression and exploitation. They keep their eyes fixed on the height of man's destiny and on the price paid for it, and, therefore, they of all people understand the dignity of the person, and the true meaning of liberty.

6. The champions of the people against God are the worst enemies of the people.

7. There are only two principles of good government: authority and counsel. There is only one foundation: justice.

Islam

1. The issue of salvation is faith in God — Incarnate. The Church must reach the Moslems with this message, even if it has to pay the price it paid to convert the Roman world.

2. Ever since the rise of Islam the religious strategy of the world remains unchanged: Christianity is contained within an Islamic zone which prevents the evangelization of the rest of the world.

3. Missionaries at different times, but especially since the time of Saint Francis Xavier, have gone around the Islamic wall, but have not yet succeeded in establishing permanent Christian societies. The growth of the Church must be continuous, and, therefore, we cannot ignore the Moslem world.

4. Before the Incarnation, infidelity meant, on the whole, idolatry; after the Incarnation, it is iconoclasm.

5. Islam cannot be dismissed as a military conquest: where are the conquerors before and after? It cannot be dismissed as a philosophy: what philosopher dominates the lives of so many people in so many countries and for such a duration of time? Only the Semitic genius for religious intensity, and the tradition and prestige of Abraham could begin to explain the fact of Islam.

6. The non-Jewish sons of Abraham, who continue to form the core of Islam, have indeed much of Abraham's faith and spirit, but not the central object of his devotion, for Abraham saw (in prophecy) the days of Jesus and rejoiced.

7. Islam cannot be converted by inter-faith; nor can it be won by hypocrisy.

Pantheism

1. The essence of idolatry is the attribution of divinity to a creature. Pantheism, therefore, is in the highest degree idolatry: the attribution of divinity to the creature as such — to nature. An idol remains an idol, even when it is an abstraction.

2. Pantheism is the philosophy and religion of Asia, the one continent not yet penetrated by Christianity.

3. If we do not convert distant Asia to the Faith, it will eventually overrun and undo the Christian West with its Pantheism. As a matter of fact it is already doing that through Freemasonry.

4. There are more pantheists than atheists. Pantheism is a subtler, if at times less violent, danger to the Faith.

5. There is another way of bypassing the divinity of Jesus than outright denial, and that is to make everybody and everything divine.

6. The very first sentence of Revelation confutes both atheism and pantheism by affirming the reality of God and declaring the world a creature. At the same time, the very fact of revelation is a confutation of deism.

7. Lucifer is not an atheist. He is proud, but he is not a fool. Lucifer is a pantheist who thought he could be like the Most High.

8. The wisdom of Lucifer gives to pantheism a unity and purpose far beyond the wisdom of the world and of the flesh. It is a fake wisdom, of course, but it is the most perfect imitation of the true one. Lucifer can, and often does, turn himself into an angel of light.

9. Pantheism flatters nature while it eliminates grace.

10. When unrestrained by the disciplines of faith and sound philosophy, science tends to deism, but poetry and art to pantheism.

The Book of Nature

1. The whole world was created for man: very little of it for his use, and all of it for his instruction.

2. Jesus, the Eternal Word through whom all things were made, taught in parables; that is, pointed to the wisdom that was hidden in things from the foundation of the world.

3. Nature is God's art, meant to lead us to contemplation. Human art presupposes and imitates nature. Some art aims at utility; all art aims at contemplation.

4. Things closer to us, being more intimate and more familiar, (like salt and the mustard seed) are not less objects of contemplation for being also useful. Some values can be taught only by things utterly useless, like the stars.

5. Flowers are reflections of eternal beauties on the flux of time. Different flowers, by something innate to each, suggest different values (love, sadness, modesty, purity, aspiration, etc.). Trees teach us the beauty of life and of growth, and specific trees seem to be the incarnation of human feelings and human ideals. The mountains are teachers, and so are the rivers and the seas; so are the days and the nights, and the seasons; so are birth, sickness and death . . .

6. Even ordinary household objects are our teachers; they are also fitting objects for our contemplation. Doors teach us courtesy, patience, hospitality; clothes teach us modesty, purity, elegance, dignity, consecration; tools teach us poverty. Work days teach us joy and dedication; feast days teach us joy and devotion.

7. One grain of sand could teach us the mystery of creation, of existence, of purpose, indeed, the secret of the universe.

Freemasonry

1. We are the Church Militant. This means that a war is on. How can a man be a soldier of Jesus Christ if he knows neither the enemy nor the issue?

2. The Freemasons, in accordance with their allegorical rituals, are Gentiles working for a Jewish end. Why should a true Gentile Christian desire the rebuilding of Solomon's Temple? It is fulfilled now and replaced by the Church. What it stood for, when it stood, is the exact opposite of what it means today. It stood for faith in Jesus Christ.

3. I do not know if Freemasonry is a religion, or if it has a consistent philosophy. But it certainly has a plan of action aiming at the destruction of the supernatural order (the Faith and the sacraments). Like a snake in the grass it is mostly hidden, but you may detect its presence, and sometimes even perceive its fangs, in the suppression of religious orders, the secularization of education, the legalization of divorce and other immoral practices, the depreciation of dogma and the ridicule of liturgical rites, the promiscuous mixing of religions, and the general paganizing and Judaizing of society.

4. Liberty, equality, fraternity; here are three values presupposing the great fact which gave the world Christianity. In their Christian context (the dogmas and disciplines of faith), the three combine to produce a force consistent, constructive, and creative. But in the faithless Masonic context, the combination is destructive. A society that is free will not long remain equal; and a society that is guaranteed to remain equal cannot be free. Whether you sacrifice liberty for the sake of equality, or equality for the sake of liberty, in neither case is the resulting society truly fraternal.

5. True brotherhood is only of those who recognize a common father and a common mother. In the natural order, there is a kind of metaphorical brotherhood of those who have a common motherland. Human solidarity has for its basis our common rational nature which transcends all brotherhoods and is not exclusive.

6. Every duty creates rights, and every right, duties. But the highest right proceeds from the first duty: the duty to save our souls. Those who possess this right are equal; those who exercise it are free; those who apply it to others are fraternal.

The City of God

1. The City of God has never been and can never be a full reality on earth; but it has once been and could become again an effective ideal.

2. Every individual soul is a little realm where all things can be made to conform, without limits, to God's plan, for that realm. This is sometimes referred to, metaphorically, as a city of God. But properly speaking, the City of God is a social thing. It involves the public recognition of God's plan.

3. The City of God has been subverted, not as a reality, which it never was, but as an ideal, which it must always remain. It has been subverted by superficial science and false philosophy, but above all by souls become cynical and irresponsive to issues of justice.

4. The foundations of the City of God include, not merely the universal desire for the Good, which is always with us, but a clear perception of the True, which can never be taken for granted.

5. God's plan cannot ignore the natural order. For the natural order provides necessary grounds for the edifice of grace. God gave us the true religion to guide us to our supernatural destiny; but the true religion must be freely chosen and assented to and served in a rational and just society governed by the natural law, known and respected by all men of naturally good will.

6. Two varieties of wisdom ought to be cultivated in the City of God, the wisdom of faith and the wisdom of reason. The latter is the same as true philosophy, or *philosophia perennis*.

Royalty

1. For the management of temporal affairs, nations can choose between different forms of government; but all must belong to a kingdom, if they choose to be citizens of heaven. For the first proclamation of the Gospel was in these words: "Repent, for the kingdom of heaven is at hand." (Matt.3:2)

2. Those for whom utility is the supreme value can hardly explain this fact, but to the contemplative mind, it could not be otherwise.

3. The symbolism of royalty is necessary for the life of the spirit.

4. In the kingdom of heaven the subjects are the nobility; rather more, they are their heirs.

5. When Christian kings lost this ideal, they became the disciples and allies of their worst enemies. One of the graces that accompanies fidelity to God and to His Church is the gift of the discernment of spirits.

6. God's implicit covenant with Christian kings: Honor Me in My Church and the people will honor Me in your persons.

7. God gives the people wise leaders as a reward for the public recognition of His authority. This is providence.

8. God discovers the one loyal heart in a contemptuous nation, but public favors must have a proportionate cause.

9. It is consoling to know that the kingdom of God is in our hearts; yet we continue to say in prayer, "Thy kingdom come!"

Our Lady

1. All religions claim to bring us to God; but Christianity not merely claims, but actually has brought God down to us. The effective difference between the Christian truth and all false religions is the Blessed Virgin Mary.

2. All the distinguishing marks of Christianity reflect our Lady's image: the Mass, the sacraments, the idea of purity, the beauty of family life, chivalry and the elevation of womanhood, the sanctification of body and soul, and the nobility of the meek and humble. I see the image of Mary in these, and in thousands of other Christian values.

3. It is only through Mary that the mystery of the Blessed Trinity was clearly revealed, and that the revelation was made understandable and lovable. The complete revelation of the secrets of God had to await her personal advent. A girl must be her own revelation. No message or figure will do.

4. Mary is the universal mother of the life of grace, as Eve is of the life of nature in us.

5. Without Mary, no Incarnation; and no ultimate and satisfactory answer to the question: Why did God create anything at all?

6. Ideals are ideas we think about; Mary is the ideal who thinks about us.

7. All the virtues of Christianity subsist in Mary and become personal. She says of herself: "I am the Immaculate Conception," and we say of her: "Thou art our life, our sweetness, and our hope."

8. Love of Mary, is love by Mary, is Catholic predestination. Those who are not attracted by Mary have hearts whose affinity is hell bent.

9. What could arouse every thought, value, or emotion in us, more than the very notion of a Virgin Mother!

10. Seeing with the eyes of faith, Mary with God in her arms is the essence of all orthodoxy. All heresy is in the beclouding of this vision.

11. From the first verse of scripture Mary is dawning: we call her God's masterpiece of creation. The world as a creature must give credit to its maker, and can only do so fully when Mary takes the center. Then, every existing entity acquires a new value as of the background.

12. We call Mary the "Mirror of Justice": That is, the perfect image of the Eternal. The eternal Father delights to contemplate His resemblance in a daughter; the eternal Son, in a mother; the eternal Spirit, in a spouse. These most intimate relations to the Godhead constitute the fullness of grace. No mere creature could be more God-like. The Daughter is immaculate; the Mother is intact; the Spouse is glorious. For a mind, once elevated by grace to the contemplation of such realities, to descend lower is the beginning of apostasy.

Saint Joseph

1. It is frightening to think of how much God entrusted to the care of this one man — Joseph.

2. The whole of the Old Testament leads up to him: this is the first lesson of the New.

3. We must think of Joseph as the wisest of men: a blend of work and contemplation.

4. His only utterance in scripture is the holy name of Jesus. Having been chosen to proclaim officially the name of the Savior, this wisest of men desired that no other utterance of his be preserved.

5. Saint Joseph is still somehow the head of the Holy Family.

6. Saint Joseph lived under the Herods! Happiness and holiness do not depend on external circumstances. Those who truly want to be saints can achieve sanctity anywhere, anytime. The worse the circumstances, the greater the challenge and the opportunity. Some martyrs who suffered under the persecutions might not have saved their souls in times of peace.

7. It is the love and devotion of the faithful that discovers Joseph, the great treasure. Outside the Church he means nothing: is not even an issue. Inside the Church, devotion to Joseph is a measure of loyalty.

The Apostles

1. The Apostles were charged with one assignment: to teach and to baptize all nations. Since the Church is apostolic, this is still its one assignment.

2. All that is naturally good helps towards the fulfillment of this task (law and order, good sound thinking, natural virtue, worldly peace) but no natural good can be a substitute for it.

3. Establishing throughout the world, in all nations, the same faith, the same sacraments, the one true Church docile and obedient to the pope — this is the work to be done. Any other endeavor not leading to this is at least a distraction.

4. The prime effect of the heresy of Liberalism is the destruction of the apostolicity of the Church.

5. The Masonic project to unify the world along naturalistic lines is a continuation of the human project about the tower of Babel. We must aim at the supernatural unity of the City of God — the only cosmic unity that has the blessing of God on it.

6. The first truth that ought to be discovered by the natural mind is the paramount right of the true Faith to be taught in every human society. This should have been the first article of human wisdom of the natural order. This should be the first constitutional principle of International Law. The Apostles should have been received by the nations as the benefactors of humanity that they are. But men possess a fallen nature and, therefore, every one of the Apostles suffered martyrdom.

7. It is a sin against the Faith, and a personal offense against the Savior for any one to say of any man: "He cannot be given the Faith"; yet, some one has to be willing to pay the price — as the Apostles did.

The Pope

1. The pope is the one true high priest on earth before all of heaven, the father of kings and nations, the principle of unity, truth, and order. Only God could have established the papacy, as only God could have given us the true religion. Not only should we constantly pray for the pope, but also, we should thank God for this favor: the divine institution of the papacy.

2. The pope is entrusted with the most urgent task on earth, that of leading all men to their divinely appointed destiny, their salvation. This task is not accomplished until all men possess the truth and the means of salvation.

3. There are times when the popes were able to do very little towards the achievement of their task; the usual reason is a general weakness of faith in the whole Church. There are also times when the popes, being human, have been negligent of their duty (again God allows this on account of the sins of the people). Yet, in spite of all this, without the papacy our human story is that of a jungle.

4. The world has never known a ruler so universal, nor a dynasty so indestructible. No man can change the pope or find a substitute for him. We can be free from his authority only at the price of our souls. A man can move away from under the authority of any king or bishop, but only by death from under the authority of the pope.

5. It is the most evident will of God that the whole world worship Him in the true religion under the leadership of the pope. This is the only world unity we can and must seek. All that hinders its fulfillment is contrary to the will of God.

6. The *Our Father* is an excellent prayer for the intentions of the Pope, because he is a reflection of the Eternal Father on earth and the principle and guardian of the sacramental system.

7. The general collapse of values is rooted in disloyalty to the pope by kings and leaders.

8. The pope should be revered as a father, not feared as a tyrant. The modern world has committed the sin of Cham.

9. It must be more difficult for the pope than for us to believe in his personal infallibility, and yet he must do that, like every one else of the faithful, in order to save his own soul.

10. Many doctrines of faith make harder demands on natural intelligence that those we hold in regard to the papacy, (the resurrection of the body, for example), yet not one is more evidently revealed in scripture, or more positively confirmed and consecrated by tradition.

11. Without the Pope the Church can be neither one, nor catholic, nor apostolic. It also cannot be truly holy, because all holiness presupposes the truth, and the truth of faith is safeguarded by the infallibility of the pope.

12. Many saints felt that they professed the entire faith by proclaiming their allegiance to the pope. We honor our Lord, when we declare ourselves true children of the pope; we also by the same act, champion our Lady's cause, fulfill the scriptures, and associate ourselves with the saints and with the numberless list of believers from the beginning.

Adam and Eve

1. The enemy of our salvation attacks the Faith directly and indirectly; one of the indirect attacks is the disparagement of the history of Adam and Eve. The story of Christianity presupposes that other story and is meaningless without it.

2. After their repentance, Adam and Eve, during an exceptionally long period of life, never ceased to inculcate upon their descendants: 1) the promise of a redeemer to come, 2) the supreme importance of divine worship, and 3) the great value of wisdom. The nations, all of whom without exception are descendants of Adam and Eve, in spite of all the errors into which they fell, and all the sins they committed, never failed to manifest in different degrees the formative effect of this parental influence.

3. The twelve Apostles of Jesus moved into a pagan world on the whole sinful and faithless, to announce the fulfillment of the promises originally made to Adam. Because of their infidelity, the nations found the Gospel message disturbing, yet not entirely meaningless or unexpected.

4. The whole pagan world was constantly restless, in search of a faith it had lost, and a promise not yet fulfilled.

5. When John the Baptist, pointing at Jesus, said, "Behold the Lamb of God who takes away the sins of the world," John was explaining every act of sacrifice in every nation, beginning with the religious acts of sacrifice performed by Adam and his immediate family. What else could explain the universality of that rite (the killing of animals as the supreme act of divine worship) except a common cause from the one common origin of all men?

6. The inscription to the "Unknown God," discovered by Saint Paul on a temple in Greece, and used by him in preaching to pagans, is another tribute to that wisdom of Adam, never entirely forgotten, which kept the pagans looking for religious truth above and beyond their mythologies and their superstitions.

7. Wisdom consists in a discovery of, and a conformity with, the universe, as unified, simplified, centered, made meaningful and purposeful, by the human story from Adam and Eve to Jesus and Mary.

Abraham

1. When the world had became corrupted by idolatry and immorality, and the faith of Adam and of Noe became almost extinct, God found the true faith still alive in the soul of one man, Abraham; and so God made of him a new beginning.

2. Seldom has so much depended on the fidelity of one man.

3. God called Abraham and commanded him to separate himself and his family from the world of infidelity, and promised to send the Savior from his descendants, and to bless all nations in his seed.

4. After Abraham, the whole religious story of the universe is centered in his heirs (peoples who in one way or another claim him as father). For example, the Brahmans of India told the early missionaries that they knew themselves to be descendants of Abraham, and that their secret religion was in reality Abraham's faith.

5. Abraham was a man of faith and visions. Our Lord says that Abraham saw His day and was glad. (John 8:56) The true heirs of Abraham's faith are those who accept as fact what he received as a promise.

6. And we become even more truly Abraham's heirs through that wonderful device of God's power, wisdom and love: the Holy Eucharist. For it is through Holy Communion that we become what our Lady referred to in the Magnificat: the seed of Abraham for ever.

Redemption

1. God chose to redeem us in the manner of a poor nobleman whose son fell captive. God's poverty in our world wounds the heart. He is constantly trying, so to speak, to keep up appearances. He has made Himself vulnerable and must now abide by the terms.

2. Like a man stranded who must use the remnants of the wreckage in order to restore some kind of ship, so must God make use of all that comes to hand. He undid the consequences of Adam's fall by the very outcomes of the fall: shame, suffering, and death.

3. The work of Redemption was to be not merely divine, but humanly divine, because one of its objectives is the restoration of human dignity.

4. We imitate the work of the Redemption every time we use whatever comes our way as an instrument of sanctification.

5. Jesus made it possible for us, not merely to imitate His work, but to cooperate with Him, by needing our help to reach more souls. Even our presence at Mass is made valuable.

6. Redemption is abundant with God; but He can always use more hands to pass it around.

7. Just to make another sign of the cross is to bring the work of Redemption to a new instant and to another spot.

Salvation

1. If wisdom consists in putting first things first, then a fool is one who makes salvation a second interest.

2. All the good things of this earth, including the noblest and most excellent achievements, cannot outweigh the salvation of one soul. This is the theme of all of the teachings of our Lord.

3. Restoring salvation to its proper place: this is the purpose of religion — the sole occupation of the saints.

4. If a man were to think about any other object as the saints do about salvation, he would be justly considered as one out of his mind.

5. "Jesus" means "Savior," and all Holy Scripture is about salvation.

6. Salvation belongs entirely to the supernatural order; yet in its light all natural objects acquire a new meaning, a new value, a new purpose, a new aspect, and even a new function.

7. The whole structure of religion is balanced on one sharp point — salvation. It is either the paramount objective and its means indispensable, or the pulpits remain silent, the monasteries empty, and the missions disappear or degenerate into social action.

8. Only that life is a success which terminates in salvation. In the ages of faith they asked not, first, how a man lived, but how he died.

9. It is terrible when nominal Catholics begin to live as if the infidels are right, that is, as if there is no such thing as heaven or hell.

10. The way to heaven, the only way, is the life of faith in the Church. If you propose to men alternatives, they are going to take them; but no alternative way leads to the same place.

11. Liberalism in religion is high treason — a subversion of the sovereignty of God. The way to salvation is what God commanded, not what we freely choose. God has bestowed a kind of sovereignty on the human will, but salvation is not its legitimate realm.

12. We must always remember what it took to bring the Faith down to us through the centuries. If our ancestors had kept it the way most of us today do, we would never have known what the Faith was.

13. Every Catholic we meet today is the end-point of a long line of traditions leading back to apostolic times. Any one of those lines can come to an end here and now.

14. God promised that His truth will endure to the end of time. It shall be so — through the loyalty of singular hearts.

The Cross

1. The Cross is the key to the secret treasures of the Church. A Christian is one who takes up his cross to follow Jesus.

2. The treasures of faith are hidden. How are they hidden? They are hidden under the Cross. Who would look for joy and happiness under such a symbol?

3. What is the Cross a symbol of? It is above all a symbol of disgrace before the world, of being jeered at and spit upon, of being deserted by friends and gloated over by enemies, of being in utter defeat, yet able to shout at the top of your voice: "I have conquered!"

4. Saint Paul warned us against making vain the Cross of Christ. What does that mean? It means preaching a salvation that has not got the roots nor the fruits of the Cross — a salvation without the Faith or the sacraments.

5. Only God's religion dares to take for its banner a symbol of defeat.

6. By the Sign of the Cross we proclaim the Faith entirely.

7. By the Cross we honor the true God; we associate ourselves with the work of Redemption; we proclaim the eternal destiny of man.

8. Is there any man who cannot gaze at the Cross? Is there any man who cannot pray for salvation? Is God ungenerous in His dealings with us?

9. The Cross makes our bodies pure and our souls confident; it reveals the divine meaning of suffering and of death; it lifts man to a new plane of existence.

10. When we gaze at the Cross nothing of our entire being remains untouched.

The Eucharist

1. It was when Jesus first hinted at the doctrine of the Eucharist that some of His own disciples walked with Him no more. And Jesus let it be so; for rejection of the Eucharist entails rejection of the Faith. If the Word would become flesh, we cannot set limits to His desire.

2. The Eucharist is the Incarnation extended in space and time, multiplied without being divided, reaching out to all who would unite themselves to the Son of God, the Child of Mary.

3. It is the supreme object of the theological virtues. While we live this life of the senses we cannot believe in more; we cannot hope for more; we cannot love more, than our Savior and redeemer under the guise of this sacrament.

4. The Holy Eucharist is the golden key to the mystical meanings of Holy Scripture.

5. It opens for our understanding also the book of nature. Even ordinary things, like fruits and flowers, and ordinary processes like the communication of life and the sustaining of life, acquire a new value, a deeper meaning.

6. The Eucharist and Mary rise and fall together. To eucharistic Christianity, Mary is indispensable.

7. To heretics, Jesus is "the good master." What master gives himself as food to his disciples?!

8. According to Saint Thomas, Jesus in the Eucharist hides His humanity as well as His divinity. It is to reappear alive in His saints.

9. All our faith, all our duties of divine service, all our treasures of grace, are now contained in this littlest of packages! Everything else of Catholic life proceeds from It, even unto art and architecture.

Loyalty

1. To be at peace with my king's enemy is nothing short of treason. Pacifism in the Church Militant is more than gross neglect of duty. It is a stand disloyal to our Lord and our Lady.

2. Part of the virtue of loyalty is a love, an appreciation, and a protection of all other fellow combatants who are also loyal.

3. Liberalism, the heresy of our day, is fundamentally a crisis of loyalty — note the sworn hatred of liberals towards those who are still loyal.

4. God never deserts a loyal heart: "*Et pia corda non deseris.*" What a consoling thought — to one who is truly loyal.

5. Loyalty is the captain of the virtues of religion and will need each and every one of them: courage, prudence, intelligence, wisdom, subtlety, great love and devotion and dedication, detachment and mortification, humility, trust in God, great faith and hope and charity; but above all, the indispensable companion of loyalty which is the virtue of vigilance.

The Parables

1. Jesus taught with parables. The littlest things, which were never thought to teach, revealed the deepest lessons of wisdom hidden in them from the moment they were created. God the Father hid those treasures there, and God the Son revealed them.

2. "The kingdom of heaven is like unto a mustard seed". "Behold the lilies of the field!" "If the salt should lose its savor" With what infinite tenderness and gratitude did Jesus use these allies in conveying His message.

3. Good will, purity of heart, and genuine interest in salvation are all that is needed to understand the parables of our Lord. Much more is necessary for the understanding of any human science.

4. Failure to appreciate the parables is a mark of diabolical pride.

5. With Jesus teaching, the world becomes one big eloquent testimony to the highest wisdom.

6. Along with this new humanly divine method of sublime teaching, Jesus also revealed the new economy of supernatural life: "For he who has, to him shall be given, and he shall abound." (Matt. 13:12)

7. Jesus came to make God more knowable, not more obscure, and for this purpose every object in existence was ready to be of service — it was meant to be so. This is the point of the parables.

8. What great surprise when men heard for the first time that the kingdom of heaven is like to a net cast into the sea!

9. The parables teach us the contemplative aspect of the universe.

Profession of Faith

1. The Faith must be professed in every generation as if for the first time.

2. We learn from Holy Scripture that those who profess the Faith will always suffer persecution; but also, that they will shine like stars for all eternity.

3. The martyrs of the catacombs professed the Faith in their time; this is why we have it today. But every new age is a new area, and a new promise of other victories.

4. The same Faith has to be professed today in the face of new enemies and other problems. The martyrs of the catacombs never heard of Theosophy or of Dialectic Materialism.

5. The true meaning of *Agiornamento* (updating the Church) is that we should be demolishing the idols of *today*, rather than that we should be offering incense at their popular altars.

6. "He that heareth you heareth me," says Jesus. (Luke 10:6) And the people said of Him that He spoke as one "having authority."

Death

1. While Christians continue to use the same common names as other men, yet for them nothing is truly the same: this is especially true of "death," for Jesus has transformed its nature by a kind of divine alchemy. Death is now the beginning of true life for those who die united to Jesus.

2. At the thought of death our whole being is torn between grace and nature, because by nature we must continue to dread it.

3. The saints were eager to die. Some martyrs did not even realize that they were undergoing their passion, on account of their great ecstasy.

4. Our Lady chose to die. Death is, therefore, beautiful and pleasing to God — the testament of humility.

5. Saint Thérèse considered love for death a measure of faith and of sanctity.

6. Catholics live for a good death, as unbelievers live for pleasure, power, or popularity. Every *Hail Mary* is a prayer for a good death.

Heaven

1. We have only one business on earth: to make earth our way to heaven.

2. No human act is truly virtuous unless it can bear this label: "heaven-bound."

3. Wherever we are, whatever we may be engaged in, heaven must remain our direction.

4. All natural virtue must be raised to the order of grace; otherwise, it has nowhere to go.

5. Every act of creation is accompanied with an intention. For an intelligent creature, the difference between heaven and no heaven is the same as the difference between fulfillment and frustration, or between success and failure.

6. To reach heaven, we seek God, follow after Jesus, imitate the saints, join the society of the angels, live loyally, and die well.

7. The *Our Father* and the *Hail Mary* are prayers for heaven. "Our Father who art in heaven . . . Thy kingdom come . . . Pray for us, Mary, now and at the hour of our death."

8. If going to heaven is the greatest good, then showing the way to heaven is the greatest work of charity.

Hell

1. It is possible to imagine a hell that would be incompatible with a merciful, or even with a just God; but that would not be the authentic hell of scripture, of dogma, and of faith.

2. The essence of hell is the loss of the Beatific Vision; therefore, it is the loss of something whose very reality is known only through faith.

3. Even in hell, not only the justice and wisdom of God, but also His mercy and love must be in evidence. This we cannot see now, but we will see in eternity. No one is punished in hell beyond the measure due to his sins.

4. Where sufficient awareness exists of the danger of being separated from God for all eternity, no other punishment of hell need be emphasized; but the fires and worms of hell must be preached where weakness of faith or its complete absence make light of the loss of God.

5. Without the Faith, the best that our nature would desire would amount to nothing better than a comfortable hell. This is actually most peoples' conception of a heaven.

6. The first effect of the action of grace is to give us holy desires: hungers and thirsts for things far above this world and all that it can offer.

7. The men of holy desires, alone, understand.

The Blessed Trinity

1. We know God from reason as the Creator and First Cause of all things. We know God through Revelation as the Blessed Trinity; the Father, Son, and Holy Spirit, one God. The Trinity we adore as Christians is not other than the God we know by reason, but involves another and more intimate (or more personal) manner of knowing the same God.

2. Knowledge of the Trinity of Persons in God is the essence of Christianity. It is also the foundation of our hope. From what we know of God by reason, there is an infinite chasm between us, hopelessly unbridgeable. The revelation of the Trinity is the revelation of our opportunity. We can become sons of God. There is such a thing. It is not meaningless. Our hope is boundless. Creatures (as we truly are by nature) can become divine by grace. The sharing of divinity is already an eternal fact.

3. Natural theology, that is, the theology of unassisted reason, does not fully satisfy our spirits. It raises as many questions as it answers. It does not answer the urgent question: Why did God create the world that we know? Indeed, why did He create at all?

4. If the inferior order of being, which is the inevitable result of an act of creation, cannot be made to tend toward an infinite goal, God would not have a motive for creation worthy of Himself.

5. It is true that we cannot reason to the doctrine of the Trinity, but until that doctrine is given to us we cannot have peace—not the peace that the world promises, but the peace that can be attained only through grace.

6. Without the knowledge of the Trinity, no other Christian doctrine is even meaningful. It is only where the mystery of the Trinity is preached and dogmatically defended, that we can hold to the Divinity of Jesus, the Divine Maternity of Mary, the Real Presence in the Eucharist, the power of the sacraments, and the eventual reality of the resurrection of the body and life everlasting.

7. It is only through the name of the Blessed Trinity that the "voice of rejoicing and of salvation" is heard in the land. (Ps. 117:15)

All Things Work Together (Rom. 8:28)

1. These are evil days! Yet what is there to prevent anyone from loving God like Saint Francis, Saint Theresa, or Saint Agnes? Why not start now?

Other Loreto Publications

Admirable Heart of Mary
St. John Eudes - $24.95
Being and Knowing
Frederick D. Wilhelmsen - $16.95
Catena Aurea 7 book set
St. Thomas Aquinas - $99.00
A Commentary on the Book of Psalms
Saint Robert Bellarmine
Hard Bound - $79.00
Soft Bound - $49.00
Continuity of Religion
Bishop Bossuet - $19.95
Cosmology
Br. Francis Maluf, M.I.C.M. - $17.95
The Devotion of the Holy Rosary and Five Scapulars
Fr. Michael Müller, C.SS.R - $14.95
The Sources of Catholic Dogma
Denzinger - $29.95
Douay-Rheims Bible
$44.95
Fish on Friday
Fr. Leonard Feeney - $14.95
The Gift of Self to God
Fr. Nicolas Grou, S.J. - $9.95
The Holy Mountain of La Salette
Rev. William Ullathrone - $14.95
The Immaculate Conception of The Mother of God
Rev. William Ullathorne - $15.95
The Intimate Life of Saint Thérèse
Fr. Albert Dolan - $29.95
Introduction to Philosophy
Br. Francis Maluf, M.I.C.M. - $9.95

The Life of the Good Thief
Msgr. Gaume - $14.95
Liturgical Year 15 volumes
Dom Guéranger, O.S.B. - $219.00
Little Pictorial Lives of the Saints
Fr. Alban Butler - $19.95
The Mass
Adrian Fortescue - $18.95
The Medal or Cross of Saint Benedict
Dom Guéranger, O.S.B. - $9.95
The Miraculous Medal
Jean Marie Aladel, C.M. - $12.95
The Mystery of the Crown of Thorns
A Passionist - $17.95
Our Glorious Popes
Sr. Catherine, M.I.C.M. - $12.95
Papal Monarchy
Dom Guéranger, O.S.B. - $27.95
Roman Martyrology
Third Turin Edition - $22.95
The Sacred Heart of Jesus
St. John Eudes - $15.95
Saint Cecilia
Dom Guéranger, O.S.B. - $29.95
Spirit of Solesmes
An Anthology - $19.95
Treatise on the Spiritual Life
St. Vincent Ferrer - $4.95
Why Must I Suffer?
Fr. F.J. Remler - $9.95
The Wondrous Childhood of the Most Holy Mother of God
St. John Eudes - $14.95

Other Loreto Publications

INTRODUCTION TO PHILOSOPHY
BROTHER FRANCIS, M.I.C.M.

In imitation of Saint Thomas Aquinas, Brother Francis teaches the wisdom of natural philosophic truth under the light of supernatural revelation. After "the Word was made flesh and dwelt among us," there is no other way to teach natural wisdom except as the "handmaid of theology." This *Introduction* is meant to whet the appetite of those who seek to know the higher things in order that they may love the same in the Most High. Each discipline has its own chapter: Logic, Cosmology, Psychology, Ethics, History of Philosophy (Part I & II), Epistemology and Ontology (Metaphysics). Great for the higher grades in "home schools" as well as for those adults who have never studied philosophy.

Sewn-softbound 188, pages, $9.95

COSMOLOGY
BROTHER FRANCIS, M.I.C.M

Without sound philosophy to set the limits of scientific inquiry and regulate its modern tendency for cosmological usurpation, science degenerates into scientism. God is the Creator of the universe. All things are ordered to His ends. All matter is at the ultimate service of man's supernatural vocation. This course was given in the spirit of Saint Thomas Aquinas, the "Doctor of Creation." Nature and the fidelity thereof, matter, space and time, substance and accidents, wisdom and the laws of nature, unicity and the four causes, and finally, the culminating chapter on the final cause, or teleology (purpose) of things, make a captivating study for every man and woman who wishes to be childlike and repose in the contemplative embrace of wonder.

Sewn-softbound 390 pages $17.95

BEING AND KNOWING
FREDERICK D. WILHELMSEN, PH.D.

This book contains twelve philosophical treatises by Doctor Frederick D. Wilhelmsen. The essays of this book were not written for students of philosophy as much as for masters already occupying chairs. Written as a challenge, an assault upon the modern world of undisciplined thought, *Being and Knowing* is a creative metaphysical exercise in the art of clarifying the deepest and most fundamental ideas. Dualism, in any form, simply has no leg to stand upon against the logic of St. Thomas and his modern "interpreter," Frederick Wilhelmsen.

Sewn-softbound, 232 pages, $16.95

www.loretopubs.org

Other Loreto Publications

THE SACRED HEART OF JESUS

SAINT JOHN EUDES

Like St. John the Apostle, St. John Eudes had the privilege of what could be nothing less than direct intimate access to the Sacred Heart of Jesus and the Immaculate Heart of Mary. One can only conclude after reading this book on the Sacred Heart that here was more a seraph than a man, driven by the Holy Spirit to cast the fire of the Savior's love upon this earth with the pen of a scrivener lost in divine abandon. Surely, our Lord gave the key to the treasure house of His Heart to St. John Eudes. This book opens that treasure to the one with holy desires.

Sewn-softbound, 183 pages, $15.95

THE ADMIRABLE HEART OF MARY

SAINT JOHN EUDES

What this seraphic father, St. John Eudes, achieved so prominently was to build a structured edifice of enduring devotion that modeled the admirable heart of God's own Mother. Eudes reveals to his disciples this most pure and maternal of all hearts both in its corporal and spiritual pulsations, while demonstrating with a dozen unforgettable natural and scriptural analogies how this human heart was so inexhaustibly divinized by the one Divine Heart of God the Father, Son and Holy Ghost. *The Admirable Heart of Mary* was given to us from the Cross by Jesus Christ that it might be honored, cherished, invoked and, ultimately, with that of her Son, reproduced in them. This is the essence of the spirituality of St. John Eudes.

Sewn-hardbound 402 pages $29.95

THE WONDROUS CHILDHOOD OF THE MOST HOLY MOTHER OF GOD

SAINT JOHN EUDES

Although by no means a private revelation, this labor of love, written by St. John Eudes almost seventeen hundred years after the holy events, reads as if the mind of the saint was guided and protected from error by the Mother of God herself. Never, in the history of the Church, had any tribute to our Lady's childhood been composed which so marvelously applies so many texts of Holy Scripture with sound Catholic doctrine and the wisdom of her confessors. Where do we begin if we are ever to become like the little children God wishes us to emulate? Why not begin by contemplating the immaculate life of the precious and most humble maiden of Nazareth.

Sewn-softbound 290 pages, $14.95

www.loretopubs.org

Other Loreto Publications

THE LITURGICAL YEAR - 15 VOLUMES
DOM GUÉRANGER, O.S.B.

This monumental liturgical work, comprising fifteen volumes, was the life-long labor of Benedictine Abbot Dom Guéranger. Written with the heart of a seraphic contemplative, the holy abbot takes the reader on a daily spiritual pilgrimage through the liturgies of both the East and West. Truly here is a priceless treasure awaiting your holy exploitation. Such was the strategy employed by the father of Saint Thérèse of Lisieux who made it a daily routine in the Martin home to read to his five daughters from these very volumes.

Sewn-hardbound, with satin ribbon page markers;
15 volumes over 7,300 pages $219.00

THE MASS
ADRIAN FORTESCUE

Father Fortescue skillfully demonstrates the continuity of religious ritual rooted in the Holy Sacrifice as ordained by the Eternal High Priest and Victim, the Lamb of God, Jesus Christ. The one Sacrifice, liturgically re-presented in an unbloody manner, always maintained the same essential form whatever the time or place it was offered in the Catholic world. As this great scholar proves in this admirable study, all Catholic rites come from the same apostolic parentage. If you love the holy Mass, you will find this book a worthy companion to your missal.

Sewn-softbound, 428 pages $18.95

THE SOURCES OF CATHOLIC DOGMA
DENZINGER'S ENCHIRIDION SYMBOLORUM

In this age of doctrinal latitude and speculative innovations there is a need for a comprehensive source book on authentic Catholic dogma that is magisterially anchored, while at the same time both practical and non-voluminous. You have such a book in this English translation of Denzinger's *Enchiridion Symbolorum et Definitionum*. This collection of articles of faith and morals has had universal appeal and approbation since the pontificate of Blessed Pope Pius IX. The edition being offered here by Loreto is that issued in 1957. The collection includes all the early creeds (symbols) of the Catholic Faith beginning with that of the twelve Apostles, all dogmatic definitions stamped with the Petrine authority of the Apostolic See (*ex cathedra*), decrees of the solemn magisterium, papal bulls, encyclicals and letters.

Sewn-hardbound 715 pages, $29.95

www.loretopubs.org

Other Loreto Publications

FISH ON FRIDAY
FATHER LEONARD FEENEY

The words, spoken or written, by a soul that genuinely loves God have a tone which always rings true. Couple this truth with literary genius, deep spiritual dicernment, and childlike simplicity and and you are describing Father Leonard Feeney, the author of *Fish on Friday*. Loreto Publications is delighted to put this American Catholic classic back in print. Too many generations have been deprived of Father Feeney's winsome literary sagacity. "Long before he ran into a bit of trouble, from which it was obvious that he would recover, given his whimsical sense of humore; Fr. Leonard Feeney, S.J., wrote some of the most delightful things ever published in our land. *Fish on Friday* was one of the best. It first appeared 60 years ago, and never a Lent goes by with out m renewing my friendship with it. . ."

- John Cardinal O'Connor

Sewn-hardbound, 166 pages, $14.95

GIFT OF SELF TO GOD
FATHER NICOLAS GROU, S.J.

This monograph, composed by Jesuit Father Nicholas Grou, is the fruit of a pastor of souls well acquainted with the strategems of an adversary determined to get the focus of battle-weary Catholics off the straight and narrow course leading to personal sanctity. *Gift of Self to God*, the heart of the composition, is a provoking and healing meditation dealing with man's absolute obligation, and salutary necessity, of giving his whole mind, heart and soul to God. It is a perfect compliment to the spirit of Saint Louis de Montfort's *True Devotion to Mary*.

Sewn-hardbound 88 pages $9.95

TREATISE ON THE SPIRITUAL LIFE
SAINT VINCENT FERRER

A written work of any saint is a desirable possession. A book written by one saint and endorsed by another saint is doubly precious. Of this *Treatise* St. Louis Bertrand did write: "Nowhere have I ever seen virtue painted in such bright colors as in this book." This is not a book to be read by the fainthearted. It was not written by a man interested in impressing anyone on this side of heaven. The *Treatise* is adaptable to all who wish to strive for perfection. This work must be digested rather than just read.

Soft-bound, 58 pages, $4.95

www.loretopubs.org

Other Loreto Publications

THE MYSTERY OF THE CROWN OF THORNS
A PASSIONIST

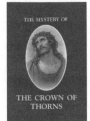

Laurels of praise would have contrasted sharply with the crown of thorns our author so cherished; yet he is deserving of gratitude by those in the Church Militant seeking the narrow way to eternal life. The path was laid out to a fallen Adam when God cursed the earth: "thorns and thistles shall it bring for to thee." From the many figures of the crown of thorns in the Old Testament to the reality of that instrument of torture beaten into the adorable head of our Savior, this book will help us to understand something of the mystery of sin and the awsome price the Just One had to pay to conquer it.

Sewn-softbound, 302 pages, $17.95

THE LIFE OF THE GOOD THIEF
MONSIGNOR GAUME

This is the story of the "first" thief, whose wonderful eleventh hour conversion and defense of the holy Kingship of Christ on Calvary merited him the everlasting title, "The Good". Monsignor Gaume opens his story with a description of the life of a highway brigand in the days of the Caesars. He presents the meeting of our thief and the Son of God in Egypt on the occasion of the flight of the Holy Family from the sword of Herod. The rest of the story is the story of the Passion as seen through Dismas, a man dying on a cross with Christ, whose only request to his "Lord" was but a "remembrance" in His Kingdom!

Sewn-softbound, 208 pages, $14.95

WHY MUST I SUFFER
FATHER F.J. REMLER

Whether it be due to our own over-indulgences in abusing the goods of this earh, our transgressions againts God's command-ments, or the providentially paternal designs of our Creator, we will have our lot of Sufferng in this life. There is no escaping that. Suffering and death are part of our debt due to original sin. Father Remler provides fifteen reasons why we ought to embrace our tri-als and tribulations, be they physical or spiritual, for the opportu-nity that every pain provides us to be made conformable to the Man of Sorrows. This practical book has a foolproof game plan that, if followed, will cut short, or even cancel our time in purgatory.

Sewn-softbound, 96 pages, $9.95

www.loretopubs.org

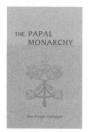
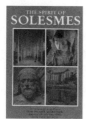
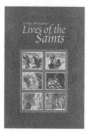

Other Loreto Publications

THE ROMAN MARTYROLOGY
THIRD TURIN EDITION

The Roman Martyrology was a written catalogue of those saints who shed their blood for Christ during the early centuries of pagan persecution. When she triumphantly arose from the catacombs, the Church introduced other great saints, who were not slain for the faith, into the *Martyrology* as she combined the recorded *Acta* of both east and west. These pages contain the names of thousands of our most valiant Catholic heroes and heroines along with a very brief biographical sketch. As an official book of the Roman liturgy, the *Martyrology* is read during the canonical office of Prime and at the evening meal in the refectories of most monasteries and convents.

Sewn-hardbound, 384 pages, $22.95

THE CONTINUITY OF RELIGION
BISHOP JACQUES BOSSUET

This history of the true religion, written some three hundred years ago by Bishop Jacques Bossuet, is a study of the Old and New Testaments in the light of God's interactive and faithful presence. There is no book which better explains the meaning behind the types and figures of so many commandments given to the patriarchs and the prophets of old by the Lord God. No book better illustrates God's particular and permissive providence in the rise and fall of nations and empires. As you read this book you will understand how it is that nothing of the ancient covenant was left unfulfilled in Christ and/or in the Church. This is scriptural theology for clergy, religious, or laity.

Sewn-hardbound, 272 pages, $19.95

OUR GLORIOUS POPES
SR. CATHERINE, M.I.C.M.

"I could not put it down!" Enthusiastic responses such as this are typical upon reading this written history of the Church as illustrated in the challenging pontificates of ten of her greatest champions of orthodoxy. One is taken on a journey through four hundred years of *tempus ecclesiae*, from the momentous entrance of St. Peter into the fearsome capital of Satan's doomed empire, to the triumph of the Council of Chalcedon, held under Leo I. Vividly brought to life is the maturation of the Church Militant from its infancy in Jerusalem. The remaining bulk of information dovetails into the major periods of religious crises and tells of those heroic popes who steered the Church through these gravest trials.

Sewn-softbound, 266 pages, $12.95

www.loretopubs.org

Other Loreto Publications

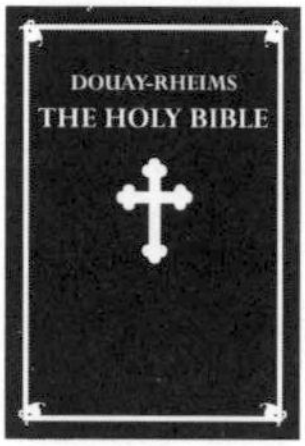

DOUAY-RHEIMS HOLY BIBLE

LEATHER-BOUND

Even after all of the modern "revisions" of the bible that are available to Catholics, the Douay-Rheims version (the only Catholic English bible in use for almost 400 years) is the very best produced. We, at Loreto, are now offering this beautiful leather hardbound gift edition! This bible is very popular — it fills the great need for a small good quality Douay-Rheims edition which has not been available for many years. It is a perfect gift for Christmas, First Communions, Confirmations, weddings, birthdays, etc., and it is also great for those who want a portable bible which is very durable.

1,392 pages with maps, index, and 32 illustrations; God and red satin ribbon page markers
Sewn-leatherbound, $44.95

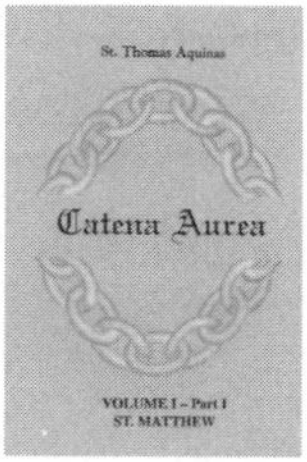

CATENA AUREA

SAINT THOMAS AQUINAS

The Dominican Tomaso d'Aquino, composed this *Catena* at the behest of Pope Urban IV. *Catena Aurea*, or the "Golden Chain," was not the title Saint Thomas gave to his work, nor were the gospel commentaries his own. Rather, they were a collection, or anthology, scrupulously collated and organized by him, but written by others — the fathers and doctors of the Church. Also, with the thirteenth century and the Byzantine reunion with the Papacy, came a huge treasure trove of expositions from the eastern fathers never before utilized by western theologians. Saint Thomas' assignment was to prepare for publication this universal wealth of holy erudition. He did so, as only a Thomas of Aquinas could.

Sewn-softbound, 4 volumes, 7 books, $99.00 set

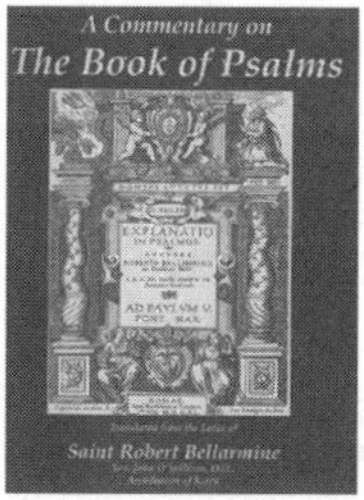

A COMMENTARY ON THE BOOK OF PSALMS

SAINT ROBERT BELLARMINE

To exhaust his intellectual and devotional energies in writing, Saint Robert Bellarmine prepared for posterity his very own commentary on each of the psalms. "Most of the Psalms of David," he wrote, "read like a compendium of the whole of the Old Testament, a summation in poetic capsule." Others (Ps. 2, 21, 44 & 60) speak so clearly of Christ that they seem rather to belong to the Gospels. Yet, it is not the royal prophet, rather, it is the Holy Ghost, the true author, Who desires to pluck this ten-stringed instrument of beauty called the Psaltery and bring our hearts to tears or jubilation as we sing praise to the Most High.

Sewn-hardbound, 380 pages, $79.00; Sewn-softbound 380 pages $49.00

www.loretopubs.org

Other Loreto Publications

THE INTIMATE LIFE OF SAINT THÉRÈSE
FATHER ALBERT DOLAN

Without question, the most popular autobiography of the twentieth century was that of St. Thérèse of Lisieux. Loreto is thrilled to publish Carmelite Fr. Albert Dolan's unique collection of eight monographs, each of which deals with the temporal spiritual journey of this vessel of grace, either as the saint saw herself in the eyes of God, or as she was known by her parents, four sisters, fellow religious, childhood friends, and others.

Sewn-hardbound, 398 pages, $29.95

SAINT CECILIA
DOM PROSPER GUÉRANGER, O.S.B.

In the nineteenth century there was an effort on the part of liberal revisionists to undermine the Church's history by challenging the Acts of the Martyrs. It was a righteous indignation that moved Abbot Guéranger to defend the cause of St. Cecilia, whose holy celebrity had spanned fifteen hundred years. The abbot's strategy was to validate the traditional accounts of all the martyrs' lives by exonerating just one. He achieved this, in the holy virgin Cecilia's case, by presenting in book form every morsel of factual evidence available, especially that which modern archeological excavations offered. As a result of his labor, there arose a refreshing new devotion to the young martyr, and the cynical scoffs of the proud were silenced.

Sewn-hardbound 406 pages $29.95

THE MEDAL OR CROSS OF SAINT BENEDICT
DOM PROSPER GUÉRANGER, O.S.B.

St. Benedict, father of western monasticism, is rather more known for his life and rule than for a medal cast in his honor. The history of the image and the exorcism engraved on the medal, as well as the power of that cross which the holy patriarch bears in his right hand, can be traced back to the eleventh century. Before he became Pope St. Leo IX, one Bruno of Toul was cured of a mortal disease after St. Benedict appeared to him in the very guise we see depicted today on this sacramental. The Sisters of Charity under St. Vincent de Paul also wore the blessed medal on their rosary. Abbot Guéranger, spiritual son of St. Benedict, wrote this book to promote this very powerful devotion.

Sewn-softbound 478 pages, $19.95

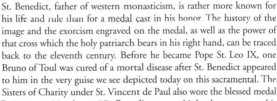

www.loretopubs.org

Other Loreto Publications

THE DEVOTION OF THE HOLY ROSARY
AND FIVE SCAPULARS
FR. MICHAEL MÜLLER, C.SS.R.

A champion of orthodoxy who dominated healthy controversy on the Catholic scene in the latter half of nineteenth century America, the Redemptorist Father Michael Müller had a secret weapon which won him more converts than did his indefatigable preaching and writing: the Holy Rosary. This book was written as a thank you to the Mother of God for graces received. Not only does Fr. Müller explain all there is to know about what the rosary is, but what the rosary should be — a sigh of gratitude. This gift from our holy Mother, he says, is a privilege to pray. After reading this devoted author, we assure you, you will never again say the rosary mechanically, or wear the scapular apathetically.

Sewn-softbound, 275 pages, $14.95

Hail Mary, Full of Grace! The Lord is with thee. . .

THE MIRACULOUS MEDAL
FR. JEAN MARIE ALADEL, C.M.

Fr. Aladel was the spiritual director and confessor of St. Catherine Labouré. The Miraculous Medal was designed by the Mother of God and communicated by her to St. Catherine with the instruction that this devotion be spread throughout the Church. The inscription: "O Mary conceived without sin, pray for us who have recourse to thee," anticipated the definition of the Immaculate Conception by nearly a quarter of a century. This book relates not only the heavenly visitations given to this humble saint, as well as her adventures and crosses endured for our Lady's cause, but also it gives the ensuing history of the medal itself with many accounts of miracles that accompanied its pious reception.

Sewn-softbound, 227 pages, $12.95

www.loretopubs.org

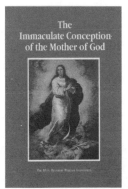